WHAT DO I KNOW?

NEW & SELECTED POEMS

OTHER WORKS BY JOHN CALVIN REZMERSKI

POETRY

Held for Questioning
An American Gallery

POETRY CHAPBOOKS

Dreams of Bela Lugosi
Growing Down
Counting Sheep
One and Twenty Poems by Grace Lord Stoke (as J.C. Rez)

SCREENPLAY

The Sandman (with Gregory Mason)

AUDIO CASSETTE

Chin Music and Dirty Sermons

EDITED COLLECTIONS

The Frederick Manfred Reader
Minnesota Poets in the Schools Anthology (co-editor)
Happy Birthday, Minneota (co-editor)
Border Crossings: A Minnesota Voices Project Reader (co-editor)
The Way Chalked Forth: A Festschrift for Elmer F. Suderman (co-editor)

WHAT DO I KNOW?

NEW & SELECTED POEMS

BY JOHN CALVIN REZMERSKI

HOLY COW! PRESS • DULUTH, MINNESOTA • 2000

This project is supported, in part, by a grant from the Arrowhead Regional Arts Council through an appropriation from the Minnesota State Legislature, and by generous individuals.

Library of Congress Cataloging-in-Publication Data

Rezmerski, John Calvin,
    What do I know? : new & selected poems / by John Calvin Rezmerski.
       p. cm.
    ISBN 0-930100-95-6
     I. Title.

PS3568.E95 W48 2000
811'.54—dc21   99-88118

Holy Cow! Press books are distributed to the trade by Consortium Book Sales & Distribution, 1045 Westgate Drive, Saint Paul, Minnesota 55114. Our books are available through all major library distributors, including Bookpeople and Small Press Distribution. For personal orders, catalogs or other information, please write to:
    Holy Cow! Press
    Post Office Box 3170
    Mount Royal Station
    Duluth, Minnesota 55803

ACKNOWLEDGMENTS

Some of the poems in this book have been included in various periodicals and anthologies. The author gratefully acknowledges the editors of those publications:

Chelsea, Collage, Dacotah Territory, Etc. A Review of General Semantics, Gustavus Adolphus College *Faculty Notes, Jam To-Day,* Mankato *Free Press, Mennonite Life, Minnesota Coalition for Terminal Care Newsletter, Minnesota Poetry Outloud 1975, Minnesota Poetry Outloud 1976, Minnesota Poetry Outloud 1977, Minnesota Products, Minnesota Times, Montevideo American-News, New Letters, Northeast, Poetry Northwest, South Dakota Review, Sumac, Tales of the Unanticipated, The Lamp in the Spine, The North Stone Review, The Wall Street Journal, Woyake.*

142 Ways To Make A Poem: An Anthology of Modern Poetry, ed. James W. Swanson (EMC Corporation, 1978); *25 Minnesota Poets #2,* ed. Seymour Yesner et. al. (Nodin Press, 1978); *25 Minnesota Poets,* ed. Seymour Yesner et. al. (Nodin Press, 1974); *Blood of Their Blood: An Anthology of Polish-American Poetry,* ed. Victor Contoski (New Rivers Press, 1980); *Common Ground,* ed. Mark Vinz and Thom Tammaro (Dacotah Territory Press, 1988); *Dacotah Territory: A Ten Year Anthology,* ed. Mark Vinz and Grayce Ray (North Dakota Institute for Regional Studies, Fargo, 1982); *Happy Birthday, Minneota,* ed. Tom Guttormsson, Bill Holm and John Rezmerski (Westerheim Press, 1981); *Knowing Stones: Poems of Exotic Places,* ed. Maureen Tolman Flannery (John Gordon Burke Publisher, Inc.) (forthcoming); *Landscape of Ghosts,* by Bill Holm (Voyageur Press, 1993); *Minnesota Writes: Poetry,* ed. Jim Moore and Cary Waterman (Milkweed Editions/Nodin Press, 1987); *Nebula Awards 23,* ed. Michael Bishop (Harcourt Brace Jovanovich, Publishers, 1989); *Remember That Symphonies Also Take Place in Snails: Selections from 25 Years of the Little Magazine Northeast* (1963-1988), ed. John Judson and Joanne Judson (Juniper Press, 1990); *Rhysling Anthology 1987* (The Science Fiction Poetry Association, 1987); *The Story in History,* by Margot Fortunato Galt (Teachers & Writers Collaborative, 1992); *The Sumac Reader,* ed. Joseph Bednarik (Michigan State University Press, East Lansing, 1997); *The Way Chalked Forth: A Festschrift for Elmer F. Suderman,* ed. David V. Harrington and John Calvin Rezmerski (Gustavus Adolphus College, 1986); *Time Frames: A Speculative Poetry Anthology,* ed. Terry A. Garey (Rune Press, 1991); *Time Gum,* ed. Terry A. Garey and Eleanor Arnason (Rune Press, 1988).

Some of the poems have also appeared in broadside or broadcast formats. The author wishes to acknowledge the Minnesota State Arts Board, the Olivia Poet in the Community Project (Olivia, Minnesota), Pennsylvania Council on the Arts, Smith Park Poetry Series (St. Paul, Minnesota), South Dakota Arts Council, and *The Writer's Almanac.*

Work on many of these poems was supported by the National Endowment for the Arts, the Minnesota State Arts Board, COMPAS, and Gustavus Adolphus College through sabbatical leaves, faculty development grants, and the college's Writer-in-Residence program.

Without direct motivation and assistance from family, friends, colleagues, editors, and audiences, many of these poems could not have been produced. The encouragement of Carol Bly, John Caddy, Phebe Hanson, Tom Hennen, Molly LaBerge, Caroline Marshall, and Joe and Nancy Paddock has been especially valuable. The author owes particularly large debts of gratitude to Bill Holm, longtime companyero on the quest, to Rob Gardner, a wonderful director and wise counselor, along with the members of the I Got Lips You Got a Tongue All God's Children Got Lungs Hallelujah Poetry R Us Chorus, to all the brave poets of Minnesota Poetry Outloud, to Jim Perlman, for his kindly and tough-minded commitment to making this book be the best it could be, and to the late Frederick Manfred, who made clear why it matters whether we write.

To Lorna—
to love and be loved

CONTENTS

Introduction   *x*

from HELD FOR QUESTIONING

Genesis	18
Facts of Life	19
Animism II	20
Elegy for Spectators	21
Courtship and Conquest	22
The Fugitive	23
Visit	24
The Best Policy	25
Fall Morning	26

from AN AMERICAN GALLERY

Superhighway	28
Why Henry Thoreau Never Married	29
Dr. Williamson	30
Willmar at Night	32
The Baptism of Annie Johnson	33
For Martin Luther King, Jr.	35
Grandfather	36
Grandmother	38

from DREAMS OF BELA LUGOSI

Section I	42
Section II	44
Section VIII	47

from GROWING DOWN

Way Back	52
Cherry Pop	53
Bone Song	55
The Radio Says	57
Alarm	58
Growing Down	59

from REDREAMINGS

A Dream of Heredity	62

Ecological Dream   64
Alcohol and the Intellect   65
Misdirection   66
A Long Dream   69

from CHIN MUSIC & DIRTY SERMONS

Chin Music   72
This Business of Desire   74
If You Ever Remember Me Loving You   76
Playing Touch   77
Wind Song   78
Soul Auction   79
The Bebop Era   80
A Little Chin Fugue   83
Family Music   84

UNCOLLECTED POEMS

Heyoka Ceremony   88
Tarzan   98
Alien   100
Your Voice   102
Marie   103
Second Marriage   106
What the Grass Knows   107

NEW POEMS

A Small World Modified   110
Consumer Education   111
All Night Truck Stop   112
Love on the Rocks   114
Original Sin   115
Of All Possible Worlds   116
The Music That Is Everywhere   120
Dance   122
Flying Over the Top of the World   125
A Gift of Two Stones   126
Devotion   127
Grave Thoughts   129
Sea Chanty   131
Popeye   132
Morning on the Prairie   133

INTRODUCTION

When I began writing this introduction, I had not intended that it become a manifesto. I wanted to explain what my literary values are, who has influenced me, and how my writing has developed over the past thirty years.

I wanted to explain, for example, how William Stafford always left me shaking my head at some bit of wisdom it seemed I should have always known. Once, after I had placed a new premium on clarity in my poems, I attended a workshop Stafford was conducting. He asked what criteria we used to judge good writing, and I raised the standard of clarity as an essential quality. He said, "Yes, but we have to be careful not to think that our clarity is God's clarity." *Nor the reader's clarity,* said a voice inside me, reaffirming my growing conviction that a poem is not an artifact to be preserved in a library like a museum exhibit, but an act of communication in which readers need to be consulted.

Or how in 1966 Robert Bly helped me understand that the everyday and the surreal support one another, subverting consensus through imagery. My poem "Visit" resulted from his insistence that a prosaic comparison between a peeled orange and a planet should be experienced as an image rather than merely stated as a metaphor. The earliest version of the poem concentrated on a topographical comparison to a globe. Bly urged me to consider the image as a point of view, to recall the stimulus that had provoked the comparison. In this case, it was seeing the light from a fireplace illuminate an orange in a way that reminded me of a planet shown on *Star Trek.* His nudge to my imagination made me put my eyes in the position of a starship orbiting a world, prompting me to bring the world to life. The imaginative rush of discovering that poem led to the generation of many more poems, and also harmonized very well with my long-standing love of science fiction and fantasy, opening my imagination to allow them into my poems.

But the process of explaining what I do and why has also led me to consider questions to which I have not articulated responses before, and I have to confess that I am somewhat surprised by the direction it has taken, and by how strongly felt some of my ideas appear to be. I have also been somewhat startled by the continuity of my ideas. However, I want to clearly state that my poems do not proceed from any literary theory. I have plenty of literary opinions and preferences, but like Stafford with "God's clarity," I am suspicious of opinions that apotheosize themselves into theories.

The punning title of my first book, *Held for Questioning*, announced a set of persistent themes in my writing: struggle against efforts to imprison those who question received truth; questioning not as mere casual curiosity, but as a mutual embrace of the world; and, not least, a sense that we all have some kind of information important enough to merit inquisition. I suppose it also reflects a view of creativity—that questioning is the spinal cord linking body and brain, knowledge and imagination.

This book covers the questioning I have experienced in the intervening years. *What Do I Know?* is intended as an open-ended question, not as enunciation of a know-nothing point of view. It is not meant as a fashionable post-modern acknowledgment that we can never really know "the truth," nor is it a lament for bygone certainties. To ask "What do I know?" is not to surrender, but to take stock. It is an opposite to "What do I care?" It reflects determination to find a coherent view of life even though we are chronically short of sufficient data, to care enough about our fellow beings, to have enough passion for the world, to seek ways of affirming ourselves and each other.

The poem "Consumer Education," where the question occurs several times, shows it as an attempt to understand a complex interplay of circumstance, motive, compassion, and an economics that should include beauty, emotion, and morality in less superficial ways. The question becomes a white cane with which to negotiate a sane path through a cockeyed world where neither compassion nor philosophy is much esteemed. It becomes a key with which I can open a gateway to empathy when "there is nothing here I could change but my presence."

Asking "What do I know?" only works to real advantage if we do it continually. It should not be understood as "What have I concluded?" It is first a way of discovering the gaps in our understanding, and thereafter a strategy for filling in those gaps. We tend to rush along until we encounter a gap, then frantically look for a way to leap over it. If a heroic leap is not possible, we muster our determination, and try to build a bridge. But a gap in understanding is not like a physical canyon; why not fill the gap rather than circumvent it? We cannot fill it with things we already know. Instead, we must begin questioning and fill it with things we have not already been conscious of. "What do I know?" leads to "What do I need?" and "What must I do?"

We watch the world at work, and through questioning, learn where we fit into that work—discovering day by day, dream by dream, question by question, that our place changes every day. "What do I know?" has been for me a way of coming to understand the universe as my true community. The question does not demand a single answer, but requires a list, a catalog, a request for suggestions, as well as changes of mind.

From 1967 through 1977, I did extensive research into the Dakota Conflict of 1862 and set out to write a book of poems exploring the historic resonance of that war as it related to the pervasiveness of violence in American culture. The working title was *Blood Medicine.* Try as I might, I could not get the collection to work as a unified book, so I abandoned it, and published some of the poems in magazines and anthologies. I had earlier resolved not to produce poems attempting to speak from a Native American perspective, though I had already written a few such poems. This decision was not due to political correctness—I strongly believe in the power and integrity of imagination in respect to cultural emulation, but I recognized that Native American writers who were coming to greater public attention at that time could speak more imaginatively and eloquently about that sad history, and had a prior right to be heard.

Thus, most of my poems about the 1862 conflict reflect the points of view of the white participants and their descendants. A few of the *Blood Medicine* poems appear in this book, including "Heyoka Ceremony," about which I am ambivalent even though it has been praised by reviewers. The thoughts and actions I attributed to the executed Dakotas were based on contemporary accounts, and are not my invention. Reading *Through Dakota Eyes* (Minnesota Historical Society Press, 1988) has made it clear that my sources were not adequate. I include the poem here because it is a critique of history, an attempt to ground historical events in the conflicts between feelings and ideals, which I regard as one of the essential obligations poets have toward their own cultures.

One of the defining experiences of my poetry career was my eight-year association with Minnesota Poetry Outloud, which in the 1970s took groups of poets to communities all over Minnesota, performing poetry and music in libraries, parks, nursing homes, senior citizens' centers, day care centers, bookstores, churches, saloons, local festivals, and wherever else we could find an audience. We often held open readings for local poets, and encouraged our audiences to present their own favorite poems.

I undertook a careful study of our audiences' responses to poetry. I discovered that people's tastes were a good deal more sophisticated than we had expected, and that while their initial expectations were often narrow, their tastes were catholic. I also learned that poems could be simultaneously introspective and conscious of the audience.

From that experience I received a whole new set of goals for my work. I had already thought of poetry as essentially an oral art (and I think that reading poems aloud until we find the right voice for them is the very best way of understanding them), but now for the first time, I felt I could write poems directed at real audiences, rather than hypothetical audiences, at audiences drawn from broad communities rather than audiences only of fellow poets and academics. I had been set on this path years earlier by my teacher David Ignatow, who had prompted me to value my working-class upbringing while opening my poems to the irrational and to social concerns, and by Bill Holm, who had enticed me away from the academic posturing of my early poems, and who has continually prodded me through advice and example to refresh my language.

In Poetry Outloud, and during years of readings in schools, libraries, jails, and arts programs, by 1982 I had read to more than 700 audiences, from pre-school children to centenarians, from scholars to day laborers—audiences of varying genders, races, ethnicities, occupations, positions of authority, varying degrees of good will, drunk and sober, fundamentalist and atheist, willing and unwilling, bigoted and apathetic, urban and rural, families and orphans, sleepy and freshly caffeinated, raucous and reverent. And I had learned that while most of them were responsive to poetry, many of them wished they could write it, and a few wanted to devote their lives to it, they all wanted to be in it or wanted their experiences, emotional and physical, to be in it. I can't count the number of times someone has come up to me after a reading and said, "I've got something for you to make a poem out of...."

I assigned myself to put more different kinds of people into my poems, to expand the range of experiences and feelings I would write about, and to elaborate my poems with whatever linguistic resources seemed likely to engage my audiences with the content of my poems. I found I could not simply develop "a style" or rely on a single voice; the poems needed to find their own voices. I also found that incorporating elements of popular culture into poems provided audiences allusions more revealing than literary allusions (though I like to use literary echoes as well). In recent years I have been writing mostly prose poems and poems containing musical effects. In 1993 I used some of them in a live-to-tape radio show, *Chin Music and Dirty Sermons*. I should add that while I enjoy writing poems that experiment with sounds, it is equally important for me that those poems say something—perhaps about religious politics ("Soul Auction"), aesthetics ("A Little Chin Fugue for J.S. Bach"), or both ("The Bebop Era").

Since 1974, almost all of my poems, even those addressed to particular individuals, have been written carefully to be heard. For me, poetry is grounded in actual voices speaking of real experiences and of the imagined experiences generated by feelings.

William Carlos Williams said, "No ideas but in things." I would add, "No feelings but in bodies." I confess that I am a materialist, not in that caricatured and trivialized sense that gives preachers, teachers, and social critics straw men to unpack for material to stuff their own shirts, but in the sense that I believe that the material universe is sufficiently explainable in material terms. A mystery is no less powerful to us at the moment just because its ultimate explanation is physical rather than metaphysical. My early education conditioned me to be as vulnerable to superstitious feelings as the most avid animist, but for me those feelings are consequences of the unexplained, not explanations of natural consequences.

Nonetheless, people often tell me how spiritual some of my poems are. I rarely object, but do not encourage them. Events or images from the poems may incite feelings that some consider spiritual, but which I consider to be expressions of "transcendental materialism." By this I mean that various concatenations of material nature and culture can lead us to ineffable feelings and consideration of so-called higher truths. Oddly enough, that same process often leads to humor (not the humor of jokes and irony, but the humor of recognition, of seeing our own images distorted in the looking-glass of someone else's words or actions). Some of my poems are humorous in this sense. Some others, like "Grave Thoughts" and "Morning on the Prairie" are pure examples of transcendental materialism. I acquired transcendental materialism from reading Whitman and Shakespeare during my formative years.

Of course, all our years are formative, and what we form out of words, whatever world and works we choose to mirror or to examine under the lens of language, makes us who we are, makes poetry of our own lives and each other's, and fills the poems with a spirit that is a pure distillation of the ways we rub against each other, bodies and words. I say, "You believe in what you want to believe in. I would like to understand *you* as much as I believe in myself and the world we must help each other to understand."

—John Calvin Rezmerski
Eagle Lake, Minnesota
December, 1999

from

HELD FOR QUESTIONING

1969

GENESIS

Stories of creation
written on the belly of an old woman—
stretch marks like butterflies
flapping as she turns, bends,
laughing at children laughing
at things on her face
they do not know she is not ashamed of.
Laughing too at her holding hands
with the old man with tired pockets,
the two of them children together
laughing.
She bears children in her sleep,
he teaches them how to dream:
children laughing, eating apples,
not smelling what he smells,
the sweat of the land coming out of the apples.
He thinks of the children copulating,
she of them laughing, not cruelly.
Do not chide the children,
they are remembering things before they happen.

FACTS OF LIFE

Daughter, let me warn you
as early as possible.
You are not
to pay any attention
to Scott Richardson.
I see him,
and you not yet a week old
and sleeping,
running his hands over your legs
in a way ill-becoming
a two-year-old.

ANIMISM II

This bench is alive.
My father made it.
The table is dead;
we bought it that way
to put things on.
I have a candle.
It lives,
when somebody lights it.

Nobody lights the sun
but it is alive too,
because nobody buys it.

My father told me
some people buy other people.
Somebody should go light them.
People are not
to put things on.

ELEGY FOR SPECTATORS

Facing someone else's death
in the back room of a respectable place
is no time to feel a fever.
You measure the temperature of your mind
in sins above normal,
there is quick significance
in the length of your bones,
you match one leg against the other,
listening for pains in the marrow.

A corpse says nothing about agony,
less about a vague ache in the throat.
The other visitors among the flowers
seem to hear something you missed.
They pass it along: life goes on, life goes on.
The murmur echoes back from the lilies
so softly only you hear the change:
goes off, goes off.

COURTSHIP AND CONQUEST

So I told her what I wanted
and bang, across the face.
If that's the kind
I thought she was,
I could leave—now.
Shocked, utterly shocked.
How could I?
Never mind the kisses,
between friends;
I should have my hands lopped off
like a long-ago thief.
She was a cat
with her tail trod on;
at my car she grabbed my arm,
said she loved me, don't go.
It was the same thing
every time,
all the way to the altar.

THE FUGITIVE

What if after all these years
in the same body,
I turn out to be somebody else?
What a new thing
to decide which pair of pants.
How sweet to have grapefruit
and like it for the first time.
I would burn old letters,
buy a new toothbrush,
learn to like the closeness
of cold on my clean skin.
I would pronounce every word
as though it were fine glass.
It is an old story
I tell the mirror
while I gape at my teeth
looking for someone else's cavities.

VISIT

A peeled orange is like a world
my eyes fly around,
scanning gold mountains
and white rivers.
Who are its people,
and do they mine pulp
or drill for juice?
What is their gross national product?
I wonder if they know about
the seeds in their planet.

THE BEST POLICY

If Christ cut down the cherry tree,
there would be no fuss about lies.
He would chuck the axe in the Potomac,
set the tree upright, take a bushel
of cherries to his father, saying:
I have done something wrong; these
should not have been picked out of season.

FALL MORNING

Standing in the fog by the highway,
I can call the passing trucks ships;
standing in the fog, alone,
nobody has to believe me.

from

AN AMERICAN GALLERY

1977

SUPERHIGHWAY

Interstate 80
crosscountry
at sixty or seventy
the road is strewn
with woodchucks
crushed
skunks squeezed into one last spray
possums sleeping in blood
foxes gone to dark red
deer here and there
sometimes
a porcupine or rabbit
or a scattered bird
you can't tell what kind at this speed
and once in a while
the busted body of a person
someone who dared
step far enough into the past
to set out along the road on foot.

WHY HENRY THOREAU NEVER MARRIED

Something about a woman
is green and secret
like a pod of beans.
So I began by studying
beans,
folding back the shells
looking for seeds,
splitting open each seed
looking for the soul of the bean,
looking for some reason to say
women are holy.
I thought to start
I could pick them over,
plant them, harvest them,
go out in the field and sit with them,
cut away the clutching weeds around them,
handle them, finger them,
take them to my house,
talk to them,
taste them, sort out
the sweet and the starchy.
I could give each one a separate name,
I could know all their secrets.
Cell by cell,
I could know them all.

DR. WILLIAMSON INSTRUCTS THE ARTIST CONCERNING HIS REPRESENTATIONS OF THE SIOUX

I will paint them running,
they are like deer.

No, no, no, no,
the missionary tells the artist,
Don't compare them with animals.
They are like children.

Spoiled children, says the artist,
I will paint them shouting.

No, no, no, no,
They haven't had your chance,
they lack the means . . .

And the conscience, says the artist,
I will picture them with drawn knives.

No, no, no, no,
Even a savage knows righteousness and wickedness.

Especially wickedness, says the artist,
I will show them dancing wildly.

No, no, no, no,
In another generation
they will be as good as civilized.

When the sun is rising
we all claim to be westerners.

WILLMAR AT NIGHT

I have been to Willmar, Minnesota,
where the houses look pious.
At night they hear noises,
metal wheels squeaking and hissing,
the throb of engines biding their time.
The houses turn over in their sleep,
dreaming of following boxcars,
windows wide open, wind whupping
through parlors and bedrooms,
finally, in Fargo or St. Paul,
letting strangers enter
with whiskey and loud stereos.
I have been to Willmar, slept in Willmar,
crossed the tracks in Willmar at night.

THE BAPTISM OF ANNIE JOHNSON

1. Among a clump of humid Christians
in a yard on Seventh Street,
she and grandfather
have sense enough to sleep.
It's a good day to be saved,
dressed in bleached cotton,
white and wrinkled in her basket
like a chestnut in its husk.

She has been washed and exposed to strangers
while a radio sings hymns to industry.
She will hear the different ways
of holding a pencil,
and which one is right.
Here is the visible church.

2. She has faith in milk,
but mother is among the guests.
Older children are next door
swiping apples
to throw at each other.
She wants to know
forgiveness
but grandmother
steals all of God's attention
with a gouty foot.
Clouds pile up in the West,
lightning tickles the horizon.
She begins to cry;
sin or no sin, she's hungry.

3. Her thunderstorm is ready.
Water hits her harder now.
We file into the house,
bearing ham and potato salad and cake
and children
as though boarding the ark.
She cries as though
afraid for her life.

FOR MARTIN LUTHER KING, JR.

After all the formal baptisms of water,
without ceremony
he entered the Jordan of his own blood.

We have been looking for gurus
to move quietly among us
and have not heard the thunder
of souls breaking out of bodies.

Life and death are on television,
dancing
in the words of followers and leaders,
electric and indistinct.
CBS and NBC cannot weep. In their pictures
even tears seem black and white.
No blood drips from the screen
onto my living room floor. Yet,
I walk around it. Lord,
I say to someone I have never seen,
Make me transparent.
Make us all transparent.

GRANDFATHER

At your anniversary Mass in July
the holy water was polluted
and nobody noticed.
Fewer of your friends came out this spring,
and Grandma wilts a little each summer
with the beans and the tomatoes.
The garden is played out,
even the worms don't go there so much.
The only thing that has stayed the same
is the smell of the sulfite smoke
from the paper mill
and it no longer smells like money.
There is a stairway to your porch now,
and a hole between dining room and kitchen
to pass cups and dishes through.
I bet there is an old quart of peach brandy
in the cellar, and a tobacco can
hidden with some emergency money forgotten
while you waited in bed for your heart to quit.
It is your voice I remember best,
still half Polish,
and the roughness of your faced black sweater.
Remembering your whiskers on my cheeks
makes me feel like I'm six again.

The family never gets together
to play Pinochle any more.
The chicken house is empty,
even the dogs are gone
that stayed there when the last chicken was eaten.
It seems to me you used to keep pigeons.
Grandpa, if you had known my God
he would have protected you from yours.
He would have.
Your children are prospering
and you have dozens of great grandchildren.
Since you died we have acquired new one-way streets
and another stoplight.
And they're finally going to pave your street.
And according to the papers
Poland is still there.

GRANDMOTHER

In her house I learned to listen to seashells.
The house full of the smells of raisin bread,
chicken soup, blackberry wine,
lavender sachet, laundry bluing, and coal smoke.
The smell of work.

Bronchial pneumonia is a dying old person's
best friend, according to the doctor.
106 degrees for three days,
but cold hands.
She seems to remember everyone all right,
but who know what she knows,
who knows what she forgets?
"What do you think of an 80-year-old woman
having a baby?" she asks.
"I'm beautiful," she says.

It's finally her day off.

Her homemade rag rugs
lie on the gray linoleum,
the blank TV faces potted plants.
Her wedding portrait rests in the closet,
young and narrow-waisted, holding
blue carnations.

She comes forth like a flower.
And withers.
Blue carnations in her casket,
rosary in her hands:

her last wishes:

"I want my children to take
what they gave me.
I won't need it anymore.
Maybe I missed something
so forgive me."

She has stopped working.
She got sick picking up apples
on the hill behind the house
so they wouldn't rot.
The house is full of medicine
she will not need.
An electric clock buzzes.
The refrigerator hums.
I learned to listen to seashells here.

Her last confinement.
With the skill of a woman
who has done it a dozen times,
she bears down steadily,
gives birth to the spirit
she has carried full term.

Coming in from both coasts,
the family closes around her
like a flower closing for the night.
After the burial Friday morning
we open up,

enjoying each other's company
we have not had for so long,
and settle her estate in an hour or so,
and keep what we had given her,
and sing, and look
through old photographs.
And some who have been feuding
for years
sit down to dinner together.
And I listen to seashells in the attic.
She has not stopped working.
It seems as though we are
gathered around to see her new child.

DREAMS OF BELA LUGOSI

1977

I

Bela Lugosi, how much can you tell us
about Vlad the Impaler?
What do you know about being a wolf?
How much about bats?
How much about dreams?
About who you dream you are,
born Blasko Bela in Hungary?
About how you…

How who? Ha! How who?
It is the wolves.
The man in formal black
smiles:

† *Listen to Them—*
   Children of the night…
   What music They make!

He is speaking of his family,
as though the full moon
over the Carpathians
is their family portrait.
Only a moment ago
he has come down the ruined staircase
with a fat lighted candle
to greet the welcome guest
here on some matter of money
disregarding superstition.

✝ *I am*
Dracula.
I bid you welcome.

As always, he
seems to be planning something.
He has risen
with all his wolf-wives.
They have been beautiful,
buried in soft robes.
Now stoopshouldered and silent
they clutch their hands
to their stomachs.
And wait.
He needs no voice with these.
They are his as no wives
have ever been to no husbands.
His eyes
command them back to their lidded beds.
This visitor is his
alone.

　　　How you used to dream!
　　　The fan mail from women!
　　　Romantic lead in Broadway hits.
　　　Maybe, at last, a matinee idol,
　　　to make your mother proud.

Maybe it was only a crazy dream.

Poor Renfield, the madman from the Vesta,
that came in adrift with the dead captain
lashed to the wheel, the masts storm-broken.
Only Renfield left to pass for living
with his cargo of boxes marked
with the seal of the House of Dracula.
Poor Renfield, who can have no human life,
but only the little lives of flies and spiders.
Poor Renfield with his memory of
the bloodshot eyes of the vampire.
Poor Renfield, who could not trust
the gift of a crucifix. Dr. Van Helsing
tells him:

> *You will die in torment, if*
> *you die with innocent blood on your soul.*

Renfield is no longer sure he has a soul.
He has not yet had his fill of innocent blood.

> *Flies? Flies? Who wants to eat flies?*
> *Not when I can get fat juicy spiders!*

Even Renfield's laugh is the howl
of pain of a heart full of hell.

Ahaahaahaahaa!
He came and stood before my window
in the moonlight, and he promised me
things. Not in words, but by doing them.

Poor Renfield, he has so much pain he thinks of it
as a deficiency of pleasure. Blood is his opium.
Only bigger doses will make him feel better.

Rats, rats, rats, thousands of them!
All red blood! All yours, if you obey.

He should have known when he saw the horses
of Dracula's coach driven by the beat
of the wings of a bat. The Count
is his own coachman. All passengers
in this coach belong already
to the House of Dracula. In Dracula's house
you are served old wine
once. Dracula says:

✝   *I never drink*
     …wine.

In this house
the spiders play host to flies.

✝ *The blood is the life, Mr. Renfield!*

He has drunk Dracula's wine
and Dracula has drunk his health.
They have pledged something silent.

✝ *You will remember nothing...*
  I now say: Obey!

> Now he knows what no one will admit to pleasure in:
> We must devour lives to sustain our own.
> Don't let them tell you it's only a dream.

Ahaahaahaahaa!
Isn't this a strange conversation
for men who aren't *crazy?*

Remember the old woman at the inn,
offering her crucifix at dusk
before hurrying inside
behind locked doors and garlic,
saying:

> *If you must go, wear this,*
> *for your mother's sake.*

VIII

Tell us, Bela,
how you were born
near the grave of the vampire.
How you have been Dracula five thousand times,
and now know the story is true.
How as an old man you wore
a cape and the Dracula ring,
found yourself staring at the throats
of Hollywood women.
Your body was no longer your own
temple of the Holy Ghost.
You were the House of Dracula.

How exciting, to be from Transylvania.
Women find you either silly
or fascinating. The eyes. The voice.
Lucy dares to mock the voice
as she sits before the mirror combing out her hair.
Next morning, she is the subject of conversation:

An unnatural loss of blood...
On the throat, two marks...

A week later, she is the woman in white,
attacking children in the dark,
luring them with chocolate and a sweet voice.
Mina, too, has been seeking adventure.
Dracula is a frequent visitor.

✝ *To die…to be really dead…*
That must be glorious.

It is impossible to be sure when he is serious.
He cannot see his reflection in the mirror.
And he is so vain. Strolling
in a top hat. At the concert,
a perfect gentleman. He kisses
ladies' hands as one might sip liqueur.
His eyes and his voice are alike,
coals covered with ash
that makes them seem cold stone.

He hovers around women
and they do not know why,
so they wonder
at the way he stares at them.
His cold eyes warm their throats.
They do not know he has
three wives already, or is it five?
All with dry veins and empty bellies,
wandering in the mist.

What strange lies he makes women tell themselves!
Mina has been conversing with a bat,
and denies it. She, too,
has been feeling a curious thirst.

Don't let them tell you it's only a dream!
Can you see yourself clearly in the mirror,
Mina? Why are you so willing
to put away your wolfbane?
Keep your window locked!

Why does she kiss her fiance so shyly
and throw open her bedroom
to this sinister foreigner?
Does she know what *kind* of immortality
his eyes promise? Those commanding eyes,
the glowing red eyes in the mist
coming closer and closer
in the mist in the bedroom,
the mist that blends into the sheets,
his breath foul on her face,
her throat eager for strange kisses.
No woman is safe from *his* thirst.

Bela! How your mother must shudder!

WAY BACK

Sitting in a magic chair
composing my bible,
I begin
living backwards.
Moving toward my birth,
remembering less and less about death,
forgetting how to forget,
finally I am equal to anyone—
a drop of slippery water
in a velvet sack.
If you remember
reading this before,
you have not been unlearning your lessons.
You will not be saved.
Turn around and come with me
to the other end of our lives.

CHERRY POP

A woman with white hair
and wrinkles like the grain of wood
gets on the bus with an old man
who has trouble lifting his legs up the steps.
They sit together, across from me,
holding hands. One of them, or both,
smells like cherry pop. I wonder.
Maybe it is some kind of medicine.
It seems too strong to be on their breath
after a stop at a snack bar.
Perhaps it is some kind of lotion.

I imagine them naked in bed,
rubbing each other with cherry pop,
bubbles lingering on
the parchment of his belly and
under the folds of her breasts.
I see the two of them splashing
in a tub of red suds, him yelling
"Catch the submarine!" while
she laughs and rolls over like an otter.

Some days, they might use
rootbeer or cream soda.
Other days, she has a headache
or his prostate bothers him,
and they do not speak to each other
all day long,
and they keep wanting the telephone to ring,
not even thinking who they want to call.

If it were not for cherry pop,
they might never go anywhere,
might not think of anything at all,
much less that they would ever be lonely.

BONE SONG

How silently the sky is the sky
at night
like a river
full of running lights.
I can't tell
if the sky has bones,
the stars are so untidy and thick.
I'm glad I have bones,
think a lot of them.
I talk about bones to neighbors
with enough bones of their own.
They don't listen anyway anymore,
but I'm not the sky,
and can't keep my bones quiet.

Perhaps everything that moves
or makes noise
has bones.
Even a river.
Us rivers,
I want to say.
I want to reflect the sky.
I want someone to wash in me.

Attracted by my rattling,
a dog eyes me;
a dog goes after the marrow,
will work until tomorrow
cracking an entry for one tooth.

Dogs put up with meat
for the sake of bones,
the smart sound of cracking,
the fat truth of marrow-taste.
Even in sight of such keen teeth
I can't silence the bragging of my bones.

THE RADIO SAYS SOMETHING
ABOUT HOG CHOLERA AND THE
BATTLE AT DAK TO
(I DON'T KNOW ANY PIGS
BUT I REMEMBER WHAT WE ALL REMEMBER,
THAT ANIMALS WERE GODS BEFORE MEN)

Children go through life like meteors.
Every one changes more air to ash.
So little time to fret about the price of pork,
not much chance to burn candles in front of statues.
Sometimes you reach out and burn your hand on a child.
Listen to the birds again, believe them.
The sky is really falling this time.

ALARM

My son woke up at four
bitten by an elephant.
I sat up watching
in case it returned.

GROWING DOWN

If you are ten years old
I am too late to tell you
what I would have told
all you nine-year-olds:
that at eight years old
you would have been better off
if you were still seven,
but not as well off
as if you were still six,
which is when things
start to go bad:
because you are not
five anymore and
have forgotten everything
you knew at four.
So you three-year-olds
are the ones I really
want to talk to,
because you remember
what it was like
to be two-and-a-half
when people were just
beginning to talk to you
for fun, but
not baby talk like
when you were two
and they treated you
like one-year-olds.
Anybody knows better
than to talk to a one-year-old.
They don't listen

from

REDREAMINGS

1992

UNPUBLISHED COLLECTION

A DREAM OF HEREDITY

I am walking around
 with my son on my back
  and his son sitting
   on his son's back and
     I get angry
      because they
       are getting
        a free ride
         and my
          feet are
           numb.
I look down at my feet and see
   they are not moving—
     I am sitting on my father's
       shoulders and he is
         sitting on his own
           father's—we are
             midway more or less
               in a stack of men
                 that disappears way up
                   into clouds
                     like a tornado,
                       a tornado that spins
                         down to where
                           the stack rests
                             on the back of an ape who
                               is not too
                                 bright but
                                   has more
                                     good will
                                       and loyalty
                                         than I have
                                           ever felt
                                             toward
                                               him.
All around us, a mob of women locked arm in arm

shout and argue about the whole stack of us, but they can come face to face only with the ape. Now and then they try to push us over, but whenever someone pushes at the front, someone else pushes back from behind.   We are a tower, impregnable and unyielding.   They are a fierce and irresistible savanna.   The air is full of the sound of explosions.   The smell of powder is everywhere, and the astringent taste of stalemate. The battle is over. They cannot budge us and we cannot get off each other's backs. We are all paralyzed because the ape can't move. I wake up saying, "Ease off, let the ape breathe. Let me
down."

ECOLOGICAL DREAM

I am not used to driving this new car. We are sightseeing, looking for interesting farms. In the back seat, the children fight about something no adult can understand. As we round a bend at 40, I spot something unfamiliar at the side of the road. A deer? No, a buffalo. A herd of buffalo. I think I can avoid hitting them, but one steps out and cannot decide whether to cross. I hit the brake.

It stops. I swerve, it turns back. I hit it. It moves away from the front of the car. At least I have not killed it, maybe have not hurt it. I stay on the brake, but hit it again. And again. Until it is down for good and I stop and find it unquestionably dead.

I do not understand why this has happened to me, until I return to the car, shaking my head, to find all my children missing, and the countryside dead quiet.

ALCOHOL AND THE INTELLECT

My friend brushes back his dark hair, breathes on a candle. His breath ignites like a dragon's, and in a moment his whole head is enveloped in a glow the color of fire in a fireplace. Soon his entire upper body is wrapped in light, and finally his whole body exudes an aura of thin flame. He has no explanation. His wife is frightened. A neighbor suggests he has been drinking too much. He denies it.

After a while we decide it is just his blazing intelligence reaching maturity. We are afraid of him. Everyone leaves, but I can find no excuse to go. He tells me he has a rare disease: as his body deteriorates, his spirit glows with a fierce foxfire. I stay with him for hours, weeping as he becomes more and more brilliant, and he weeps too.

Neither of us can quench the flames with our tears.

MISDIRECTION

On a jumbo transatlantic plane (I think from Rome) I interview Orson Welles.

"I thought you were dead," I say. "The papers ran front-page obits."

"Yes," says Welles, "Well, I did die, and didn't they have a good time telling the world I hadn't lived up to my promise— nothing ever again as great as Kane. What part of the world cared already knew that; I knew that, Charles Foster Kane knew that best of all. He told me every day."

I say I've always enjoyed his magic on TV, and ask him if he has a favorite illusion.

"Thrills and Wonder," he says, "Thrills and Wonder, it was called. I remember asking Peter Fonda whether he had a favorite among my effects and his was The Golden Chair."

I say I've never seen it, haven't heard of it before.

"Delightful business," he tells me, smoothing his vest, "A color-changing chairs routine he described to perfection. But I'd never done it, you know. It was completely imaginary, some-thing Peter had made up to put me on the spot on a television talk show. So I pretended to remember and Peter begged me to perform it once again for the TV audience. Of course I got out of it by asking the host whether he happened to have three plain wooden chairs, one red, one blue, one green—of course not. Peter said, well, that's all right then. I have a new favorite. I like the way you've made your performance disappear.

"No malice—he meant only that performance of The Golden Chair. But I thought about that long after. Of course he couldn't have been righter. I've made my performance disappear, frittered away my talent, my money, everything but this too too solid flesh."

He leans toward me, puts his hand on my arm, pats his enormous belly and smiles. I recognize how solicitous he is being, and see that he, like me and how many more, spends all waking seconds seeking ways to please anyone who might acknowledge us with an embarrassing "thanks" or "well-done." I am warily aware that he is acting as I act when I disapprove most of myself. What misdirection: seeming aimless, as though wanting no scrutiny, using each disclaimer as an excuse to stay around those who might, for lack of any better choice, acknowledge someone half hanging back, have sympathy enough to invite a conversation, ask a question we could use to show some skill at anything at all, offhandedly as we could—some small skill, not the great work we had rehearsed who knows how long. Reluctant showoffs, afraid to show each other our best, we have a thousand favorite things to do, a particular antimasque for each spectator.

We get off the plane in New York, and I accompany him through the streets.

"Thrills and Wonder. Let's go to Tannen's* and one of us can try Thrills and Wonder."

* Tannen's: A Manhattan magic shop and mail-order supplier of conjuring apparatus and books, frequented by many outstanding magicians.

A LONG DREAM

All the people who will ever live anywhere are in one long room. I stand by the door while they file out on their way to the world. Some children first. I kiss each one, tell them I love them. They are all beautiful and the women and men who all follow are youthful and smiling and slim. I never get tired kissing billions of them and when I say I love them I am telling the truth.

Then an old man comes out. He is twisted and filthy. Putrid. His face all scarred. A running sore on his upper lip. His right eye oozing. He moves toward me in spasms. I hesitate. I hesitate.

I shut my eyes tight and kiss him on the lips, like a little boy kissing my father again in spite of his breath of stale tobacco. I put my hands on his arms. I love you, I say, and open my eyes.

It *is* my father, young as he was when I was three, as though he had been disguised to test me. People keep coming, single file, now to kiss him, not me. He refuses no one, not even those who stink or have no faces left, and I stay by his side admiring him. By the time he is done, he is old, and broken down, with a running sore on his lip.

from

CHIN MUSIC AND
DIRTY SERMONS

1994

CHIN MUSIC

When I was a little kid, every once in a while on our way home from fishing, my Dad would stop at the bar down at the Volunteer Fire Department—East End Hose Company—"down at the hose hall," we called it. I'd get to perch on a barstool and swill orange pop while he had a beer before we went home. There was always a bunch of men hanging around, usually watching baseball on the TV at the end of the bar. It seemed natural for them to be watching baseball—they had names like Shorty and Beans and Froggy and Bud. I was Lefty's kid.

There was always an argument or two going on. Usually one about sports, and one about politics. I never understood exactly what they were arguing about. Once, when we left, I asked my Dad to explain. He said, "Aw, they don't even know what they're arguing about—that's just chin music. They just like to listen to their teeth rattle."

After that, I always asked him, because I liked it when he said "chin music." He'd always vary it a little bit: "They're just making chin music. They like to hear their cheeks flap." Or: "They like the sound of their gums slapping together." I got very fond of my father's chin music. And anybody else's.

Years later, when I started publishing poems—at first, the kind of bookish poems that are hard for anybody except an English teacher to pretend to understand, my Dad would read them and shake his head. He never said it, but I could hear him very clearly: "So you're going to spend your life fooling around with this chin music?"

Chin music is like any other music—it can be played badly or well. But you like it most when you play it yourself. I learned it pretty well. Here I am getting ready to tell you about my childhood and my crazy dreams, for no good reason except that I like to hear words gurgling over my teeth like orange pop, and to hear meanings going every whichway like an argument at the end of the bar. I just like to hear my jawbone practicing the scales.

THIS BUSINESS OF DESIRE

The women in cages at the bank—
in their eyes I see someone I want to embrace.
I want to free them, saying,
as much for a laugh as anything,
"Let's take all this and go to Argentina."
But Argentina is so far away
and when I look into their eyes,
so are they, and then so am I,
so far away I do not know
what money is, or why I have come
to admire the straightness of
their skirts, the exactness of their hair,
the evenness of their thin smiles.
They seem like characters in little movies
advertising some corporation that makes
all the items we could ever want
or write a catalog about.
Their fingers sift stacks of dollar bills
and canceled checks, as though looking for
ransom notes or love letters
from General Motors or Merrill Lynch.

The smell of their perfume drifts
out the tellers' windows
and blends itself with the debts of
passing housewives in wornout coats
who carry the odor home. At night
their tired husbands smell this perfume of debt
and begin to think of escaping to Argentina,

taking along the women in cages at the bank.
I recognize the plan from old movie scripts.
I want to tell them their yearning
is not shared by the women at the bank,
who want to wash off the smell
of other people's money,
put on rumpled housecoats and be women
at home with chocolate daydreams of
ardent men, insistent as movie gauchos, who
nevertheless stick around and help with the dishes.
I want to tell them we could be men like that,
but they are so far away, I am so far away,
men and women so far away,
all of us locked in or out of cages,
going about this business of desire
with no profit, not knowing
what to save, what to spend, what to embezzle.

IF YOU EVER REMEMBER ME LOVING YOU

This poem is for you,
I want it to touch you.
Tear it out
and let it be my skin,
or
at least reach down and touch it,
along the edge,
then somewhere in the middle.
Stroke it.
Please. I want you to feel
the soft armhairs,
the callus of the heels,
the fuzz just above the tailbone,
the grainy hide over the shoulders,
the knot of the navel.
We can join skins again
as quietly as ever.
Rub this page on your shoulder,
caress your thigh with it.
Please. I am thinking right now
of your warm hiding places,
of warming your belly.
I remember you moving around me,
moving around you,
your hands
on the backs of my hands,
your fingers
light as a nightwind
through every stand of hair.
If you ever remember me loving you,
save this poem.

PLAYING TOUCH

I know how you'd like to be touched.
You'd squirm like a freshly bathed baby
feathered by unexpected fingers
brushing circles between your shoulder blades
or stroking the velvet behind your left ear.
I know you'd like your knee squeezed
if you could keep it a secret.
I know you'd like to be wrapped up
in somebody else's skin.
Me too.
I know you want to touch somebody
in the elevator
or kiss someone sitting not too far away.
Or hold somebody you know
just to see how it feels,
how warm, how fragrant, how much
like you know it would feel
if you could embrace yourself.
I know sometimes you'd like to hug a stranger.
Go ahead.
Touch somebody you don't know,
even just a finger run down the arm.
They'll think it's crazy.
I know. Me too.
Crazy as anything.
But pretty soon—
all over the world—
a family of lunatics.

WIND SONG

An invisible woman, the wind is,
all summer, caress, caress,
sweettalking the cottonwoods,
tickling the daisies, oh,
combing the grass, humming words,
the same sexy old tunes over,
mm-hmm, about naked limbs
and horny herd animals come October,
and gravid January dreams
of the zygotic April spill
of small rain and willow.
Meanwhile the days grow tumescently long,
and everything green's obsessed
by her feline rub. Ah, yes,
for a taste of her breath,
even the cool fish come up,
and waves on the lake at night
like the sighs of an anxious giant
say, Don't stop! Don't stop!
All day, birds flirt, primp,
and make impossible promises
to the invisible woman the wind is.

SOUL AUCTION

Do I hear a sinner
lemme hear another sinner
can I hear a sinner
raise a prayer
lemme hear another prayer
raise another prayer
well I wanna hallelujah
can you raise a hallelujah
lemme hear a hallelujah
raise another hallelujah sinner
sinner gonna raise a joyful noise up
can you bless the name of jesus
born once
born twice
do you know that jesus loves you
born once
born twice
give yourself to jesus
jesus loves your dollar bill
give your dollar bills to jesus
born once
born twice
born again
and again
one born every minute
sold

THE BEBOP ERA
for Philip S. Bryant

SESSION ONE

Uncle Skinny had no time for that bebop music,
which was any music he had no time for.
He grew up in ragtime times
and heard all the changes
tune by tune through tango, Dixieland, boogie-woogie,
      Kansas City, Yes, We Have No Bananas,
      Charleston, Flat Foot Floogie with a Floy Floy, swing,
      Charlie Parker, bebop, progressive jazz,
      Charlie Parker, western swing, bluegrass,
      Charlie Parker, jitterbug, Mairzy Doats, rhythm and blues,
      Charlie Parker, hillbilly, samba, cool jazz, free jazz
      calypso, folksongs, rock and roll, rockabilly, doo-wop,
      folk rock, soft rock, soul and funk, hard rock, acid rock,
      country rock, heavy metal, outlaw country,
      all the way up to bubblegum and punk and disco,
which is when Uncle Skinny was relieved to die.

Through it all, he liked Irving Berlin and
Irving Berlin, and after the War (whichever war), whatever he
heard from the radio or jukebox or street dance, he said
"I got no time for that bebop music." Ask him
did he do the Charleston when he was young,
he'd say, "I got no time for that bebop music."

SESSION TWO

He was not alone. Fathers of sweater girls
and mothers of sullen Elvis emulators
complained about rock and roll
as that bebop music, and preachers
roundly and soundly denounced
the scandalous ways of bebopping teens
while Ricky Nelson praised his Bebop Baby.
Bebop was just another name for rock and roll—
        "You call that noise music?" they said—
for any fad or phenomenon they thought was bad.
Bebop was the music to which the world
was going down the tubes
to perdition or worse.
Bebop, they'd say, is rebellion music—
it's lack of respect is why
they sing Be-bop-a-lula
and wear their jeans too tight
and shake their hips in such unseemly ways.
Playing bebop and bebop dancing
and them fancy bop-rod cars
and bopping down to the bop-shop
to have a little bop of that bop juice,
and even bebop weed at the pool hall,
leads to bopping in the backseat and
a little bebopper showing up bop-in-the-middle of the belly,
and bop gangs bopping unsuspecting non-boppers
in the alleys of our done-gone-lost-to-bebop cities.

It was all the fault of bebop.
All the fault of bebop.
All the fault of bop.
All bop's fault.
All the fault of taking bop too seriously.

Play it, says Diz, or Cannonball, or Sonny, or somebody, just *play it:*

> seedy beady bebop, reedy bebop,
> bebop a raindrop, eavesdrop tiptop atop a sodapop,
> bebop a beeboop, Betty Boop, loopity-loop, regroup,
> reedy beady bebop,
> greedy yes indeedy bebop,
> centipedey bebop,
> centipede stampede proceed
> > speedy bebop.

A LITTLE CHIN FUGUE FOR J.S. BACH

waves of	spring	floods of	auroras
mountains	alive in	snow	adrift
like	whirlpools	sleepy	dizzy
light	pregnant with	seeds of	new worlds
in columns	music and	flowers	come to visit
and arches	darkening	and water	in great wheels
in cathedrals	leaves	appear	and leave again

FAMILY MUSIC

Dad bought Mom a battered old upright
from neighbors who'd neglected for two generations
to notice it was out of tune.
They thought their kids just had no talent.
Mom had it tuned, so I began
three years of Saturday mornings
with Sister Mary Constantine.
In the convent music room half frozen
next to her grim habit,
I tried to turn dots and lines
into easy sounds of sailboats or flowers.
Her joy was the counterpoint
of my knuckles quick and red under
her baton rapping
the right time on my fingers on the wrong keys.

> "You didn't practice—it
> goes like this."

She'd elbow me to the end of the bench
and retrieve the flower music from the spinet
perfect as a funeral wreath.
I'd surrender my mother's five dollars and
run home to beg
to be allowed to quit.

> "Someday, you'll be
> glad I made you learn. Imagine
> how you'll feel when
> you go to a party and they

want you to play something."

Mom would wish again she'd gone beyond
her mere eight years of lessons.

Once a month or so
I'd come home to find her occupied
with Mendelssohn or Stephen Foster.
She'd get up red when I came in.
She never thought she was good
enough for anyone to listen.

When we moved to a new house,
the scarred piano stayed behind.

Some nights I'd lie on my bedroom floor,
ear against the radio,
jealous of a Steinway or a faraway orchestra
cutting through the static with
Beethoven or Tschaikovsky. Once my father
looked in and laughed and
closed the door.

>   "How come you're listening
>   to that
>   longhair stuff?"

He used to croon
cowboy songs while he shoveled coal.
In the tub, he'd holler Stephen Foster.

Dad did all the singing in our house, but
Mom played piano when we had one.
I never got past the second lesson book
but I learned how to listen to
somebody else's music.

UNCOLLECTED POEMS

1969-1997

HEYOKA CEREMONY

"But in the heyoka ceremony, everything is backwards. . . . The truth comes into this world with two faces. . . . But it is the same face. . . . When people are in despair, maybe the laughing face is better for them; and when they feel too good and are too sure of being safe, maybe the weeping face is better for them to see. . . . That is what the heyoka ceremony is for."

—Black Elk

1. Day after Christmas, truce over,
reporters and officers brag bodycount,
brown again this year.
Maybe they lie, or worse yet, guess.
Plain stone near Front Street, Mankato,
still brags 38 red men hanged—
that's a lie. One was white
four more were both red and white.
Buried in the sandbar, they say,
by the Minnesota River bridge—
that's a lie.
Sandbar's gone far downstream
full of sand-filled graves—
bones long washed away,
native grass dead for now,
earth under a white shroud—
not even New Years, and already
a long winter.
Bootprints from rooftops back to warehouses
left last night by the red and white man
some call Santa Claus, thinking him St. Nicholas—

Indians Christian just long enough
might have called him Waziya and thought of Heyoka—
a joke on them, but all right,
things are not as they're said to be.
The spirit of the north is the contrary spirit
as sure as the pawnbroker is the children's hero.
His footprints get smaller and smaller,
going back Christmas after Christmas
to a Christmas when there is no boasting stone
and a warehouse has been built of beams
that were the bones of a gallows.
Workers yank nails with faces of clawhammers—
with claw ends, build a gallows for 40.

2. This winter leftover Dakotas lighten themselves
for shipment to prison on Rock Island.
God has a plan to save all 300
by this penance—now is a good time
to tell them their sins.
They don't laugh at missionary talk,
they sing hymns and pray and piss
side by side and one after another,
chained leg to leg
in the yellow stained snow.
In the security of this jailyard,
the Colonel thinks,
so close after Christmas and the death of their brothers
the Colonel thinks
it's safe—
the Colonel thinks—
and perhaps only humane
to let them feel fresh air and—
the Colonel supposes—

exercise on a Sabbath morning under guard.

Saturday night a fresh foot of snow
veils the land from natives and invaders alike.
Tonight the earth has a secret life.
Impossible to find a grave tonight—
even a mass grave freshly filled or emptied.

3. Hell Sergeant
we only wanted to—
with no whiskey—
just a little fun
Sergeant, what
are we supposed to do?

You start by putting that body back,
you don't do
no shooting.
Powder's short down south.

We was just—
some targetpractice,
get us in shape for the rebs.
The body,
this red nigger
(rope burns on his neck),
just frozen solid—
ain't but
just like shooting
a statue
(gray as prettiest marble).

Found it this morn

laying there.
(one eye open to the sky)
Didn't see till I tripped
out here,
didn't figure
it was good for anything—
all frozen.
(halfway between town and grave),
Didn't think it mattered.

Don't matter.
Put it back, though.
Looks bad for the townfolk,
won't let their boys sign up.

4. Cloud-dark Friday night
one body falls off a wagon in a hurry
to the house of an Iowa physician.
This is the promised resurrection—
out of their blankets,
out of the heaped up dirt
down by the river.
The doctors come for cadavers,
free cadavers—
full-blooded cadavers,
cadavers for Christmas
The earth is vomiting bodies.

5. Friday noon, warm as Eastertime—
shovels chuck sand, jab and toss,
scrape and slap, pack,
stab and sling, trying to hit
open red mouths with clots.

A wide trench filling up,
shovel by shovel.
A layer of bodies,
foot to foot,
a layer of blankets,
a layer of bodies,
foot to foot.
Loose bodies spring off their backs
onto gray wagonbeds.
Soldiers filch relics—
a medicine bag, a crucifix,
a string of storebought beads,
a feather to tickle the trader's daughter.

A gun and shovel party in blue hats
backs jolly wagon number four
square against the scaffold.

Soon the first wagon bumps the platform,
knives snuggle back into sheaths and pockets,
corpses leap up to join neckropes
to ropetails dangling from crossbraces.
A row of puppets side by side,
lively in the wind,
clowns—
under their masks,
tongues hanging out,
eyes going yellow,
painted cheeks puffed out.

6. Hundreds of citizens go home to leftover meat
laughing about Indian antics—
Did you see that one

did you see what that one did?

Cut Nose dies,
loose rope tied quickly,
men holding his body up to it again—
the thing squirms a little,
breathes a little.
Not cooperating as usual, he
broke his rope, fell down still alive.

The crowd sucks a shout back in—
a giggle crosses the tip of a pointing finger,
leaps into the mouth of a boy soldier,
winds down to tickle his lungs,
making him tremble.

This is a mockery of the sundance—
think old warriors watching from jail—
This is not summertime,
this is not for a better life,
these are not our best men hanging there—
No one seems to be getting a vision.
We will all get sick.
The earth itself will heave.

The platform swings up
under the feet of the men,
the lock slides into its slot.
Dakota warriors let go of each other's hands,
stop straining at the ropes,
hold their heads straight up,
stand arm to arm, singing.
Long hair covered like clowns' hair,

unbleached muslin hoods rolled up
showing eyes that show hours of no sleep.

Pipesmoke funnels back into red willowbark,
words of deathsongs
swirl out of the six directions,
hitting teeth, slapping tongues
settling into bellies one by one—

Here I am,
here I am,
I am the one.
Here I am,
here I am
I am the one
who is dying today.

7. Cut Nose fastens his Christian britches,
singing—

I was there,
you will know I was there
at New Ulm, you will know
if you find a body
with its head in its crotch.

Pale women straining in the crowd
wonder why everyone says don't look.
They are too far back—
it doesn't matter much
though men laugh
or shake their heads
at Cut Nose showing off his penis.

8. A death song swoops down again.
They march backward
through the double line of infantry
shoulder to shoulder,
to be promised eternal life,
to be prayed over word by word
this beautiful Friday morning.

Running around to check his troops personally,
the Colonel says—
sending troops to keep the crowd back,
the Colonel says to the artist
from *Harper's Weekly*,
just barely made it out here in time for the hanging,
the artist says: Going off according to schedule.
Nothing can go wrong
the Colonel says—
It's discipline.
No, the Indians will not rise again,
the Colonel says—
We have finished with savagery
and they will be transported to the desert.

9. Condemned Dakotas put on feathers,
fix their hair in medicine knots,
put on paint,
get out pocket mirrors,
shake hands with reporters and officers
one after another.
Merry Christmas,
says a condemned half-Frenchman,
It's almost over.
Merry Christmas, anyway.

Merry Christmas.
Merry Christmas to you, sir,
and a happy New Year.
Nothing against you—
I only regret
I couldn't have a fair trial.
Will you take this letter
to my father?
It says I'm innocent.

Father Revaux and Dr. Williamson
have a baptism contest Christmas night.
The priest wins, 31-7.

10. The Dakotas hear the Colonel
take back the order of execution.
They hear the lies of witnesses
jammed back behind their teeth.
They go to the white chiefs
because the old men in shirts tell them
it's safer.
They don't want to give up,
back to back,
taking their axes out of the blood,
their own blood rushing in
to fill up and heal old bullet holes,
running backward from soldiers,
putting muslin back in stores,
vomiting whisky back into bottles,
man by man—
giving back treaty money,
giving back cloth shirts,
giving back hoes and plows,

anything that scars the earth.
They give back everything.
Hearing about Christmas for the first time,
they don't believe it,
and forget it,
taking back their land.
Bootprints vanish from the snow.
There is no Santa Claus,
there are no saints,
no pawnbrokers,
no missionaries,
no traders,
no debts but blood debts.
Waziya is rightfully the spirit of the north,
Heyoka is again a holy contrary
sad clown keeping evil away from good men.
They are forgetting the white man's way of making war,
the white man's way of killing gods.
They are forgetting the white man.
One by one they come back to life,
to the life of the earth.

TARZAN

Lord Greystoke caught the 4:15 elephant
home from the counting house at Opar,
after a short workout
with his daily crocodile.
At the corner of Branch and Vine
he paid exact fare (peanuts in those days),
took a deep breath of monkey-smelling air,
went up to his high-rise treehouse,
found a coconut of martinis,
had one, had another,
changed into his casual loincloth,
read the paper, asked Jane,
"What's for dinner?"
She'd lost her poultry scissors, so
they'd have to go out,
into the Village.
Dinner out for a change, maybe dancing.
Off they go to the Congo Club.
Had to sit next to a bunch of, you know,
"Knee-grows."

"This world's going to hell, by Jesus,
next thing you know, they'll be moving in
right out into the treetops,
right next door.
There ought to be a law of the jungle.
I know what I'm going to do," he told Jane,
"Get me a big lion, yessir,
keep it right out front.
Put up a scarecrow, too, show these

superstitious jigaboos
not to get ideas.
One of them bucks ever lays a hand on you, Jane, he'll
have to
answer
to Tarzan.
Personally.
A-a-a-aa-aa-aa-ee-ee-ee-aa-aa-aa-ough!
King of the Apes, Lord of the Jungle!
And don't you forget it.
Me Tarzan, you waiter—
bring me another drink, Sambo,
I feel powerful thirsty, boy,
powerful."

And everybody in the place
was
staring at him
because he was
half-naked, you know,
and spoke
with a God-awful
gorilla accent.

ALIEN

A serious ten-year old,
full of astronomy and natural history and
all his reading, without coordination,
he could explain the trajectory of a thrown ball,
but could not catch it.
Not much fun for anyone playing.
The harder he tried, the worse he did.
Gravity was in the way—
the Earth's and his own, so
he wanted to grow up to be not so human.
He was not sure of what kind of strange creature
he wanted to be, where he wanted to go,
but knew down deep
Earth's atmosphere would drug him
if he stayed here too many years.
Every night the sky was clear
he would go out in his back yard
and look for home.
His favorite star was far-
off summer-red Antares.
In winter Sirius
was more friendly to him than the eye
of any dog in town.
Somewhere in space there was an adventure
that needed a mind more than a hand, he was sure.
Or perhaps he had not yet grown
into his true form, and skill would come
as easily as a butterfly learns to fly.
If he could find a way out to the stars.

If he could discover what kind of being he was
meant to be.
                            Forty years taught him
a little dexterity with his two hands,
but didn't rid him of his sinister hope
to see four arms in the mirror
some morning. The atmosphere
of Earth has not yet put him to sleep
and he has not tired of waiting.

YOUR VOICE, OCTOBER ON THE RIVER

You sat behind me in the canoe,
doing all the paddling, except
when we hit rocks, I pushed.
All the while, we talked about
jobs, insomnia, the houses along the river.
There was white water and I laughed,
and wide bends, banks lined with bittersweet.
You told me to watch how
the light fell yellow from the trees
in beads and drizzles—
so many different sunlights!
Falling as though the syllables of your voice
had come visible!
I tried to see which flash was which sound,
but they ran too quickly into streams of light
flowing out of the pines, onto the river,
all your words shining on the water,
your voice mixing with the voice of the current,
all light and sound coming together in liquid,
going down the river with us toward sunset.
At the landing, friends were waiting
with a car. They wanted to know
what took so long. We didn't answer.
All the way back, it was quiet,
and I kept my eyes closed most of the way.
All the brightness had gone inside me
or had been left behind;
I did not know how much of each.
And I was afraid to speak, afraid of saying
something dark you might not understand
or be able to forgive.

MARIE
(FROM "FOUR GIRLS AND THEIR TEMPERAMENTAL HORSES")

Born under Scorpio,
her first love was a white horse
she saw in a book,
and later in movies and magazine ads,
the white horse everyone seemed to admire,
the white horse under the masked man,
the white horse of Joan of Arc,
the white horse with a thousand faces.
A white stallion with flame-red eyes
was what she desired
and speed that would make Pegasus
give up on his wings.
She used to go down to the high fence
at the horse-boarder's, ten years old,
watching for that white wind
that would bounce her bareback
through fields of cloud by day
and by night meadows of stars.
She watched as much as she could,
never saw him, and never told anyone
for whom she was watching.
At eleven she began to climb over,
at twelve loved the smell of the stable.
At thirteen she talked her father
into going to auctions
and from the third came home
with a mare she called Cotton.
She was Cotton's only master—
happy to have a mare, feeling

without thinking, a horse is a woman's woman.
Now sixteen, she tosses her black hair
at the men she tells
what she wants done for her horse.
Every other day, she has
a terrific craving for a ride,
feels stiff without it,
works her sluggish saddlehorse
into a lather on frosty mornings
when she rides without a jacket,
going home to wipe and brush the mare,
loving the smell of sweat and urine-soaked straw.
She loves to ride bareback for exercise,
jeans soaked, breath coming fast,
white in the chill, the calm power of
the horse rocking her pelvis,
loping along the lake where she sometimes stops
and looks into the water a while.
Sometimes in summer she camped there.
She loves the rub of the saddle
on an evening ride, doesn't mind
riding herself sore, wishing as she splashes
horse-knee-deep in and out of the water,
reins loose, horse having her own fun,
she could have the power
of the horse she wishes she had.
She wants to follow the sun
down to the Pacific, wants
to ride off into the surf at dusk,

bucking the waves all the way to Asia.
But here is the prairie, no ocean,
not even a sight of the Rockies,
no visible worlds to conquer,
no way of following today around the world.
This is not her silver stallion,
this is her phlegmatic white mare,
whose only interest in the west
is the wind they turn their backs on
headed back to the stable.
She can't forgive Cotton
her open love of home and oats.
That is why she uses her crop and heels
so hard to hurry her out
so close to sunset, when she never looks
up from the horizon at the colored clouds.
That is why she complains to her father,
"We never go anywhere,"
and makes the stablehands little promises
if they will take good care
of Cotton through the winter,
and plans grudges against them
for the end of another season of desire
when she will not have
the white stallion again.

SECOND MARRIAGE

He divorced his wife
and married whiskey,
and forgot how to fight.
He spoke less than before,
        "How are you, neighbor?"
barely remembering the names
of old friends.

After his wife left,
he began to take long walks,
some of which he came back from.
Strange little bruises
appeared on his face,
and cuts on his fingers,
and he limped as if
kicked in the shins.

Whiskey was beating him up;
unfaithful whiskey,
who had whispered
such words of love,
didn't understand him.

WHAT THE GRASS KNOWS

The grass never mistakes the moon
for the sun,
no matter how much or bright
the moon shines.
The grass is smarter
than you think.
The moon is not just for light,
but for us to
fall in love by.
The grass is smarter
than you think.

NEW POEMS
1987-1998

A SMALL WORLD MODIFIED

Hardly anybody comes here. This is just a pretty small world, dwarf trees along a narrow meandering path beside a slight stream that gurgles little gurgles as it lightly plashes over tiny rocks and rinses against the nubbins of chartreuse moss along the low banks. Petite lilies and little tiny ferns don't quite hide the pocket grottoes where the tan pygmy Buddhas sit behind their plump ceramic babydoll bellies. A little rough wooden bridge looks like a matchstick arch where the thin path threads across the water. A quite scanty cloud of nearly invisible gnats, that looks like maybe just a sun-shimmer, hangs over a shallow eddy. This is a very very small world.

Someone comes along and folds it up into half its size, and folds it again, and yet again, and still one more time, squares it up, gives it a shake, and puts it into a terrarium. It still looks quite a bit the same, only much much much smaller, and now no one at all walks the itsy-bitsy path by the teeny-weeny stream, or pauses thoughtfully to gaze intently at the eentsy-weentsy little old Buddhas, which nevertheless retain their full significance, and which continue to remind us that the whole world, big or small, is illusory.

Whoever claims this minuscule world should not become too attached to it, because it can be made smaller still, small as a photograph of it snapped by a child with a toy camera, small enough to fit into a shot-glass, even so small we can no longer see it without powerful lenses, which can also be made smaller, smaller even than the microscopic idea of the microscope itself.

CONSUMER EDUCATION

I stop at Burger King for lunch during their premium promotion for Walt Disney's sentimentalization of *The Hunchback of Notre Dame.* I sit with my burger and fries and a big paper cup full of icy cola with its pictures of a cute hunchback and a saucy Esmerelda. I am about to take a first bite when across the room I see Quasimodo. I am startled. There is a woman with one shoulder low, one high, an underslung lip, bulging brows, drooping eyes, a soup-bowl haircut. She is staring at nothing in particular. I catch myself staring and force myself to look elsewhere in the room, the table to my left, where two noisy children are examining the promotional bags from their kiddy meals, one trying to explain to the other what a hunchback is, neither of them noticing the apparition on the other side of the room. I am afraid how they might react if they notice her, that they might erupt into ridicule. Why do I not think they might simply fall silent, or say hello? I feel like I am the only one aware of everything that is going on in this commercial space, and yet, what do I know? There is nothing here I could change but my presence. And if I were not here, would somebody else come in and notice? Why do I feel so self-consciously protective of this woman who wears this face wherever she goes, and who came here of her own free will? What do I know? Would it be any different if the woman on the other side of the room had the flashing eyes and shapely shoulders of Esmerelda? The children will learn soon enough that humans come in several shapes, some of which are worth more on the market than others, and not always the ones we expect. What do I know? When I look again, the hunchback has vanished, and the children are following their parents out into the remains of noontime, one carrying a plastic model of Esmerelda, one a little figure of the evil archdeacon, ugly as sin.

ALL NIGHT TRUCK STOP

The cups of coffee drunk
to fool yourself
into finding strange and lonely places
familiar,
seeing people who remind you
of people you know
with the rattle of silver
behind their conversation.
Seeing your reflection
in the window looking like
somebody who came here to wish
he could be somebody else
here for another reason.
Through the window you can see

a man too mean to kill himself
and his wife too shy to run away
hunch over the hood of a pickup
where he draws maps in the dust.
He can find a back road to anywhere.
He lights a cigarette
and sucks the death out of it.
You got the wrong idea,

I can see he's telling her,
and can see she's not his wife
after all, but still

she's too shy to run away.

Even in a town this small,
there must be some crime.
There must be.
I used to dream of saving you
from the bad guys, I say to her,
at least it seems like you

through the thick silent window.

I guess I was just dreaming
of a job that doesn't exist.
At night, I dream; all day
I have a good-paying job.
But she's going with him.
She's going to stay with him forever.
When she dies, they'll say
her heart attacked her.

LOVE ON THE ROCKS

Sometimes he thinks he could love a stone, expecting nothing back. It would sit waiting for him to come to it, and not complain if he is early or late.

But as for his human love, whenever he approaches her, she picks up her shadow and takes her silence somewhere else. She seems to want him to change, but will not say how.

He tries to be what he would want him to be if he were her.

If he were a stone himself, he thinks, he might be more patient. But he cannot be a good stone; he is cursed by being alive. She can see that, can hear him breathing. He breathes the same air she does and she can't bear to think of her breath inside him.

He keeps trying to be a stone, trying to show how joyful the life of a stone could be, trying to tempt her into trying it herself. If only she were a stone, he thinks, I would not have to change after all. But she can see right through him; he is no good at being a stone.

ORIGINAL SIN

I remember when sex was invented. I was six the day it rained hard then settled into drizzle, and the whole neighborhood of kids seven or eight and younger went out in our swimsuits, dancing through puddles in the gutters, and two toddlers were out there naked, one a boy with his little wiggle-worm bobbing, the other a girl with a pudgy W in her crotch, and some sly neighbor-girl in a red suit started up the chant, "The boys have the wieners and the girls have the buns," skipping along the sidewalk barefoot and splashing and leading a small parade of skippers chanting along with her, boys and girls alike, "The boys have the wieners and the girls have the buns."

It was my introduction to symbolism, and when I spontaneously imagined an animated cartoon of my own wiener resting in a fresh-fleshed bun, the trickle of raindrops on my skin tickled in a new way. And some pair of mothers came out and noticed our improvised chorus and verbally snatched back their precious cherubs, including the red-suited girl, and one told the rest of us, "That's enough fun, you kids get on home and get dressed," and the other said to Buddy Karpinski, "You should be ashamed of that loose talk with girls around."

He wasn't, but I was at that moment expelled from the garden, and began my long search for a new paradise.

OF ALL POSSIBLE WORLDS

And there I am in the garden fondling an eggplant and thinking of breasts. The turnips are like hard little breasts as I brush away the dirt. The little yellow mounds of potato still buried look like the slopes of breasts above low necklines of elegant gowns. I am in a field of breasts, and when I go indoors it is as though I have gone to the home of breasts, a gallery of breasts, a museum of famous bosoms, a church consecrated to saintly breasts.

Breasts worn and unworn, wrapped and unwrapped, breasts hidden away, breasts held close, breasts freely looking out at the world, breasts that have won their independence. In books, on countertops and tables, in the refrigerator, on television, in the pantry, in boxes of candy, in teapots and bottles and bowls and candleholders and flowerpots and baskets of toys. Brown breasts, yellow breasts, white breasts, purple breasts, silver breasts, golden breasts, breasts of sugar, breasts of chocolate, breasts of flame, breasts of milk, bouncing breasts and gently swelling breasts, and singing breasts. Breasts with great brown aureoles, and pink buds, and thimble-nipples. Breasts that hang sweetly, sag, bobble, stand proud, or even seem to lift heavenward. Breasts ashamed to be breasts, that pretend not to be breasts at all, that in the schoolroom do not raise their hands or answer "Present." Breasts on vacation, or moved for good to sunnier climes.

Bras huddle in dresser drawers, treasuring the memory of breasts. Sweaters anticipate the smooth inside caress of breasts. Mirrors await their glimpses. Husbands go off to work with the cheery impressions of the breasts they saw across the breakfast table. Wives go off to work bearing their double burdens and remembering the shapes of the hands that had cupped their breasts not so long ago, and will cup them again not soon enough, or perhaps too soon, depending on whether their prenuptial agreements include the sharing of breasts.

On the street, an assortment of breasts, cosmopolitan polyglot multicultural breasts, some big enough to hold a smaller breast inside, which would hold a still smaller breast inside, and so on like Russian dolls that nest inside each other, wrapped in shawls obscuring the shapes of their breasts. Breasts walk along State Street, some bouncing, some jiggling, some dancing, some with great restraint. Some walk along as vibrant ghosts of breasts that have been given up to the surgeon, or have gone to the heaven of breasts, or have gone to be reincarnated as fresh breasts for new women. Breasts to replace breasts rest in boxes on the back shelves of stores advertising prosthetic devices.

Breasts appear in perfume advertisements, in movies, in paintings by old masters and young illustrators, in Polaroid photos, on bronze and marble statues, on novelty ice cubes, on menus, on department store dummies, on posters.

All this profusion of course is not without regard to function, the young mothers nursing at home or on the subways and in the lobbies of office buildings, their baby boys and girls, their little greedy bambini, their nipple-nibbling cherubs sucking sustenance, their eager nurslings learning that any weaning is overweening. The long history of human nourishment, which if accurately displayed would show the milk of Eve flowing through the branching tree of mothers, into their mouths and out their breasts into the mouths of daughters and out the breasts of daughters to daughters all the way down to us—us including all us dead-end milk-traps of boys whose sole function on the tree is to encourage the next round of daughters to join the great fantastic pump that is the motherhood and sisterhood that sustains what has been known for some proud reason as the brotherhood of man. Man with his little generative function in a world of breasts that both led forward and carried out the plan by which we carry on in pursuit of breasts.

In some Natural History Museum, a display makes it clear how breasts displayed as we know them are a by-product of bipedal gait. Till women stood tall, breasts didn't enthrall! Then breasts got taken for rides—on horses, in chariots, in cars, in buses, trains, planes, and trolleys, on bicycles, motorcycles, scooters, and rumor has it, brooms. All these vehicles for the convenience of taking the carriers of breasts wherever they want to go, so the inventors and conductors and paid gentleman passengers may go along the better to admire the leading breasts of the day. Breasts worn in public by the virtuous and the vain, the givers of peeks, the hiders under multiple folds of clothes.

And yet, only half the world has them, men having always to wonder why they are teased with the counterfeit coins of nipples, but having to beg, borrow, steal, or purchase the use of breasts for any purposes beyond a little titillation, for any seriously aesthetic or practical purposes. Markets and malls are full of breasts, cheap and expensive, large and small, young and old, rich and poor, religious and agnostic. Breasts proudly enter churches and synagogues and temples of all kinds. The most spectacular cathedral is but a setting for the gems of summer Sunday divine breasts.

I believe in breasts. I believe that breasts will always be present to inspire me, to comfort me, to provide me warm anniversaries, to cure melancholy of all kinds, to help me love the rest of the world almost as much as breasts, to possess me with confidence that breasts will forever and ever and ever softly and sweetly blossom in every garden, real or metaphorical.

THE MUSIC THAT IS EVERYWHERE

Walking along a hillside road near Exeter, watching jackdaws play at tumble on the gusts under off-and-on glim of spring sun upwards of a cultivated valley where Englishwomen exercise their horses in and out of shadow patches cast by low clouds— this is the same sun that once never set on the local empire, the magisterial sun so British, of Constable and Turner—bright by design, subdued by tradition.

I wish I could paint a landscape or compose a pastoral symphony.

Rounding a patch of gorse glowing yellow, I see twenty yards downhill flashes of red and white and black—jacket and jeans and boots—a dancer atop a picnic table, a woman, fair hair flying as she steps high and flings her arms to the tune of music kept from me by the earphones that make it hers, hers to keep time to, hers to spend time by, hers to keep, purchased personally from Our Price Music or Boots the Chemist's or specialty record shop, and brought personally perhaps by car, perhaps by bus, perhaps on foot, certainly right here, perhaps all over Britain and anyplace abroad she wants to go—dancing anywhere to this music she alone now owns, she alone can dance to here and now, this music unknown to watchers of her dance, ballet or boogie, visible in her visible rhythm, this individual music which is available everywhere to anyone who cares to have it and has the price—a small price for the secret of a tabletop dance in a spotlight shaft of sun in an English meadow.

And now the sun ducks into cloud, and she pauses, perhaps between songs, a brief break in that music which is available to her everywhere personally and which now prompts her to leap—leisurely jetée in white jeans—to prance and vault the low fence, scissor-kick of black boots, scarlet jacket fluttering behind in time to music I cannot hear, which is anyway available everywhere; now she is on the road led personally by that music which can be had by anyone, and she skips down the hill, leaning to one side, then the other, like a blonde baton conducting the music she carries now past the middle-aged couple with the pram, now the elderly ladies in blue coats, now the crowd of young mothers, and the couple of teenage lovers, leaving all of us pedestrians wondering what tune she hears as she struts in time, her very own tune, forgetting perhaps it is the same music available everywhere, and which we cannot hear right now, but can keep time to by the way she carries it, publicly silent, privately overwhelming, up and down the streets and valleys of any country in which we care to be citizens or visitors or dancers or watchers or painters or governors or jackdaws at play under sun which is after all as personal as our eyes.

DANCE

The little girl twirled, I remember,
years ago, through the adult room,
arms outstretched, slim feet
held near each other tiptoe
as she spun like a ballerina
fifth position on pointe,
reeling room to room,
chattering, "I'm a tornado,
I'm a tornado,"
leaving behind no damage
but a chaos of delight
in us victims of her dance.

On television I see the rubble
our bombers made of building after
building, bridge after bridge,
body after chassis after corpse,
casualty upon casualty, for reasons
they say, sufficient and necessary,
redress upon revenge upon reprisal,
cause upon cause upon causality,
whirlwind of explanation
after funnel of concussion,
after twister of diplomacy
by other means, and afterward,
a cyclone of regret,
expressed,
but:
this point, that position,

those memories
left unsaid,
unsayable,
silent.
Silent as those protesting
their makeshift quarters
in the long graves.
No tornado could do such
undoing as well as we ourselves
when we let our ethnic dances
get out of hand.

And I remember the silence
when the radio went dead
while the storm roared through
a beautiful town I once called home.
Then the racket of the saws,
the trucks, the rakes, the hammers,
the chatter of the citizens
picking up the pieces and the
challenges of their jigsaw
puzzle lives. No
storm
can match
for power
the whirlwind of the will

to rebuild, nor the desire to say
to whatever gods we care to
keep believing in, we will not
be swatted down unless
you smack us dead.
We are not victims, we are
survivors. Survivors.
Anything you can crush
we can build better.
Anything you can gash,
we can scab over.
At least that, until
we heal what we need to heal.
Yes.

The little girl has grown up
quite a dancer, and she was out there
in the whirl of mending and amending,
is still out there,
quite a carpenter in her way,
too busy making things new to worry
about a Saturday night's damage
half a world away
where someone and someone else
may be trying to find a way
to set things right again.

FLYING OVER THE TOP OF THE WORLD

"To Schrödinger, the idea of thinking about cats that are neither dead nor alive was the height of absurdity, yet. . . quantum mechanics forces us to this conclusion."
—Michio Kaku, *Hyperspace*

I wake in a plane full of sleepers—lights soft, window shades lowered. It seems we are more perfectly still than if on the ground—motionless while the world turns beneath us. I raise the shade, see wisps of cloud rushing through the fog of the headlamps. It is futile to look for landmarks in the mist, foolish to watch for mountains that drift through the sleep of passengers, bearing unpronounceable snow-covered names meaning things we cannot comprehend without lifetimes of study.

Like Schrödinger's animated mousetrap, we wait suspended to pounce at knowledge, to discover whether we will really awake in a place where no one we know will watch us come down, or whether we will be up here dreaming forever. The crew may or may not be in their box, asleep or awake. I am the only one I am sure is awake, knowing nothing of our true position, whether we have a pilot or navigator, where we are going, or why we are on this journey to a place where none of us belong, but to which we have all purchased tickets.

A GIFT OF TWO STONES, FOR MR. LIANG

"There was a wall." —Ursula K. Leguin, *The Dispossessed*

And there was a great lake that spit out agates,
layered pastries that took eons to bake,
hard and multi-hued and delicious to the mind.
Continents and seas have all they need of time,
to eat and digest and compose themselves and sleep
and spit out pretty things for humans to keep.

And the Wall, like all walls and all else
that humans cook up for themselves
thinking of permanence and safety from the new,
sooner or later comes down as all walls do.
And we might keep a fragment or two
to remind us some collapses are overdue.

We humans, each by each, have so little time
in which to wait, and only hope for enough life
to see big walls become mere curiosities.
We applaud the fall of our neighbors' walls
and hope our friend's name will be remembered,
that his family, years from now, will recall
that the latest heap of old wall was what he longed
to see, covered over with flowers layered
like an agate disgorged by a great lake,
the agate of a nation's lives, compressed, baked,
multi-hued, ancient, but tasting like open air.

DEVOTION

People on the streets of Xi'an tap their own bellies, pointing at me, and saying "Buddha." They laugh. There are so very few big bellies in China. There is the Landlord's Belly, the barrel of politically incorrect lard, subject of communist hatred, target of so much bureaucratic scorn, object of so much revolutionary derision. And there are brass or wooden or plastic Buddhas, whose rotundities people rub for luck, falling back on an old superstition after weathering so much reform that has provided them little assurance. There has been no end to reform but reform of the reformers, and reform fattens no one in public. My young guide explains this, telling me why strangers on the street keep touching my belly. "It is not just curiosity or amusement," she says. "You have the belly of the Laughing Buddha, and on your forehead, the mark of the third eye." A week later, on the bus homeward from visiting the shrine of a famous old poet restored to bureaucratic approbation, she tells me about her boyfriend, in the People's Liberation Army, posted nearly a thousand miles away these last nine months. She shows me his picture, slim and unsmiling in his starched uniform, handsome as a propaganda poster. "I hope he won't forget me," she says. Impulsively, she rubs my belly. "Now it will be okay," she blurts.

So I have the belly of the Laughing Buddha. In its next life, perhaps, it will come back smaller. But because it is respected now, perhaps it has already reached a higher plane, high above any bureaucracy. Meanwhile, it rests where it is. I sit where I sit, stand where I stand, carry it wherever it needs to go, while it helps me make my way through the crowd, fending off anyone who presses too close.

Which of us serves the other? Which of us is master? We have the perfect democratic relationship—prosperity without competition, order without anyone giving orders or forbidding happiness, perfect agreement on the correct line. No one in charge, no one losing face.

I let it pick out what dishes to eat, it lets me write the poems. We are a perfect work unit of two, with no criticism. This is not Socialism, this is not Buddhism, this is not Capitalism. It is just a belly and brain working together to make friends.

GRAVE THOUGHTS

Near midnight, three of us drive out to a country cemetery, to visit the grave of an old friend. We have soberly brought a pint of good scotch. We read names off tombstones and joke about the old characters whose lively flesh once kept all these bones upright. One friend clears encroaching grass away from the headstone while we laugh about good times together far away on a long boat at anchor under a diamond-sharp night sky. I remember lying on deck watching a satellite streak across the starfield, pointing it out to our now-absent friend, and him saying, "If I were an astronaut, I would never need to touch earth again." No spacecraft is in sight for me to imagine him piloting over our celebration.

We have come to observe an old custom. The cap comes off the bottle and the bottle tips back into the lips of the master of ceremonies, who drinks and passes it to the grave-tender, who drinks and passes it to me. The taste of the whiskey promises warmth in the chill air. I swallow, and the tickle of its bouquet rises from my gullet into my mouth and nose. It caresses my head from inside, makes me shiver. I pass the bottle back to close the circle, and my good friend drizzles the remaining whiskey over the grave. "Skaal, old sport. Drink deep," he says. It would be easy to imagine a sudden puff of breeze, a sigh coming from the grass. But it is a perfectly still night. The wet fire of the peaty malt we shared—now sinking into the earth where we know our friend is not, and filling the air he no longer breathes with its lingering perfume—is a distillation of memory and longing and grief and love and dread. It comes to me why whiskey is called "spirits." What we have done is a holy thing, a piety older than the church, older than temperance. I cannot imagine anyone coming even to the grave of an infant to perform this ceremony with milk. This is no flippancy. Milk is for this life only. Milk is of the body, whiskey a taste of another world.

SEA CHANTY

The sea is the grave that does not need to be dug. It is under-taker and leader of prayer. It is the cause of death and the reservoir of fear. It is a road wide enough for billions of mourn-ers. It is the dark place from which there is no return, and the wet place that promises endless gestation. It is the landless place stranger than any land, a country where loyal citizens cannot set foot. It is the most enduring of all earthly entities, seeming absolutely unearthly in its constant change, change, change, change, change, change, change. Storms are its little pets, and we their toys. The sea talks to us and we understand what it says too late if at all. The hissing sea, the babbling sea, the roaring sea, the sea, the sea, the ocean, the sea, the bound-ing main, the sea, the sea, the sea, playground of the tempests, looking-glass of the lazy sky, the sea, the sea, briny deep, pleated skirt of Mother Earth, Davy Jones's locker full of fresh fish, the sea, domain of Amphitrite, the sea, the sea, gaping mouth of Poseidon, the sea, deep beyond any meaning of depth, the sea, the sea that laps at the tickling toes of toddlers, chasing them back and teasing them into trying to wade a little deeper, the sea, the sea, the sea, mother of all mothers and maker of widows and orphans, separater of lovers, soft haven of hard-hearted killers, sanctuary of strange bodies and stranger temperaments, hiding place of treasures known only to uncar-ing worms, the sea without bone but full of bones, the sea, the sea, the sea, the sea, soup of everything that happens, gaming table of glaciers, repository of endless winters, rack on which ancient mariners are hung out to dry, the sea, profligate water everywhere yet nowhere for the thirsty, the stingy sea, the sea, the sea, the sea, amphora of infinite tears. . . .

POPEYE, IN OLD AGE GROWN THOUGHTFUL

The Sea Hag takes me seriously now, comes around for little debates about global warming, and the rising of the seas, and the intertextuality of the presocratics and twentieth century popular culture. I feed her cheese and tea instead of talk. She talks enough for both of us, and I don't mind listening as she goes on and on about Elmer Fudd and Diogenes. I myself am partial to Parmenides, but I hold my tongue.

I am what I am, bone and blood—all organs and no attributes. I still eats me spinach, but it does not invigorate me the way it once did. It is not what it was, and I am not what I was. Platonist no more. Everything changes and physical appearance seems more stable than feelings and ideas. People don't necessarily stay true to type, though some do.

The Oyl woman always got what she wanted, whether she knew what it was or not. I finally realized it didn't matter whether I defended her or not. I told her so. She said she didn't think it was true, but maybe it was, she needed time to think about it. We don't see each other. The bruiser who was always after her moved to greener pastures, wherever they are. I'm at the age when people expect me to say what my secret of longevity is, but I have no secret. I don't even feel old, though I know I am. I am not sure whether I have slowed down, or the world has speeded up. I no longer even *try* to step in the same river twice, but it's strange how I keep seeing the same leaves and logs drift past.

MORNING ON THE PRAIRIE

Tired of all the sameness of night in Montana and North Dakota failing to flit by my car window, I pulled over to nap, and thought I woke up in time for the sun to rise and show me more of the day before.

And I was standing on the prairie near a river facing the sunrise, and all around me the ground was alive with crickets keeping their silence in the cold and there were no cars on the highway and no planes in the sky and everything was very quiet and a long way behind me I heard the hissing of the wind in the grass, and the hum of the sun warming the flies and bees, and the far-off groaning of the mountains shifting and the pounding of the oceans on both coasts in rhythm and under all the varied rhythms was one throb as though the continent were a person dancing, fingers snapping, hands clapping, teeth clacking, throat howling, and under it all the heart beating.

Was this only make believe, or had I been living sightless at a silent movie?

JOHN CALVIN REZMERSKI grew up in Pennsylvania and is now Writer-in-Residence at Gustavus Adolphus College in St. Peter, Minnesota. Besides publication in literary magazines and anthologies, his poetry has appeared in periodicals as varied as *The Wall Street Journal, Mennonite Life, Nursing Outlook,* and *Tales of the Unanticipated.* He has long been committed to bringing poetry to non-traditional audiences, both in publication and performance. In the 1970s he led Minnesota Poetry Outloud, taking groups of poets to perform poetry and music in small-town festivals, parks, bars, churches, and nursing homes. A storyteller, and occasionally an actor, in 1993 he collaborated with a troupe of performers on *Chin Music and Dirty Sermons,* a live-to-tape radio program of his poems, sketches and stories, with music by Michael Croswell. The choral group "Pieces of Eight" performs composer Charlie Mead's settings of some of his poems. His work has earned the Devins Award, an NEA fellowship, and the Rhysling Award of the Science Fiction Poetry Association. He edited *The Frederick Manfred Reader,* published by Holy Cow! Press in 1996.